The Quirky Quiz Book for Couples

Amanda Reilly

<u>Disclaimer</u>

Table of contents

Introduction

Think you know everything about your partner? Unless you can read minds or have access to all their social media passwords, it's likely there is still many things to learn about each other.

Whether it's been 2 weeks, 2 months, 2 years or even if it's your first date arranged through the life-saving tinder app, there is always something new to learn about your partner.

If you are just at the beginning of your relationship, this eBook is going to help further develop your bond together, flourishing the passion and commitment that's already cemented your connection. Even If you have been together for years, this eBook is going to re-establish that spark, similar to the feeling of meeting for the first time.

The thirst for knowledge about your bae is going to get well and truly quenched. Through using the various quizzes inside, you will not only test how much you know about each other but also how much you have in common.

The basics
Round 1-Physical attributes
The rules

Ask your partner to close their eyes, no peeping! If they don't oblige or you think they might cheat, tie a scarf around their eyes or anything similar. Each time they get a correct answer or an answer you agree with, reward him/her with a kiss, hi-5 or a chicken nugget (carrot stick if vegan).

1. What colour are my eyes?

2. What is my height?

3. What color is my hair?

4. Name three things I might always carry with me.

5. What color is my favourite shirt/dress?

6. What color is my underpants?

7. What size is my bra? (avoid if you don't have boobs)

8. What is my best facial feature?

9. Which part of my body would you eat a salad off?

10. What part of my body am I most proud of?

That should have been a fairly easy round, now on to the next one.

Round 2- first times and first dates

The rules

This round is to be played by both of you. If you remember any of the following from your first date or first encounter then shout "yay", if not "nay". If the question does not apply, discuss if it would have made the first date better or worse.

1. Did you receive a random gift at the beginning of the date?

2. Did you hear or tell a funny joke or two when you first met? Can you remember what the joke was?

3. If it wasn't funny, did you pretend to laugh anyway?

4. Were you complimented on your attire?

5. Was your date smiling at you as they ate?

6. Did you show your friends who you were dating before the date?

7. Did you arrive early for the date?

8. Do you remember who paid for the meal?

9. Were you recommended a delicious dish by your date?

10. Did you lick a spoon at your date seductively? If a spoon wasn't available, did you just give a wink instead?

11. Did you drop any food-related innuendos during the meal such as "I like big sausages?"

12. Did you playing footsie under the table?

13. What was the first thing you noticed about your date??

14. Did you impress your date by doing an impression of a celebrity?

15. Do you remember taking a selfie together?

16. Were no phones used during the date?

17. Did you kiss on the first date?

18. Did you tip the waiter?

19. Did you go back to your date's place?

20. Did you meet again within 24 hours after the first date?

Round 3- turn ons and turn offs

The rules

Ask your partner each question about three times, they can't say anything but you have to guess whether it's a turn on or off based on their facial expression. Ask slow and sensual so it's hard for them to keep a straight face. After you finish the round, its then your turn. Winner is the person who was the best at hiding their turn ons and turn offs. We've also added a few red herrings to help you break your partner's concentration.

Questions 1-20 are for the ladies, 21-40 are for the gentlemen.

1. Do you enjoy it when I play with your hair?

2. Spend a lot of time talking with you?

3. Accommodate your personal needs such as chocolate and keeping the toilet seat down?

4. Show public displays of affection like nibbling on your ear in a taxi?

5. Do you like it when I call you pretty?

6. Do you like it when I dress sharp and make a little effort?

7. Do you like it when I smell good?

8. Do you like it when I'm mysterious, like hiding the TV remote?

9. When I talk about my hobbies?

10. How about when I whisper in your ear?

11. Kiss you on the cheek?

12. Give you a massage using my big man hands?

13. Touch you on your thigh?

14. Slowly undress you, sometimes with only my teeth?

15. Surprise you with random gifts even if you don't really want them?

16. Make you laugh by being a silly goose?

17. When I decide what your plans will be?

18. When I touch your knee under the table in a restaurant or boring event?

19. When I brag about you to friends and family?

20. When I surprise you from behind?

Now for your partner

1. Do you like it when I give you a lingering kiss?

2. How about when I sit on your lap?

3. When I show you a little skin?

4. If I have a tattoo or get one?

5. If I wear very tight fitting clothes?

6. When I'm not wearing a bra?

7. When I play with my hair?

8. Tease you with a smile then look away?

9. When I talk about my nipples being hard for no

   reason?

10. Would you like it if I watched porn?

11. Wearing certain jewellery such as ankle bracelets?

12. Heels or sandals?

13. When I recount a sex story?

14. When I wear bright red lipstick?

15. When I use my phone a lot?

16. When I wear your clothes?

17. When I tell a dirty joke?

18. Do you like it when I suck on a lollipop?

19. How about the smell of my perfume?

20. When I get my nails done and I show you several times in the hope you notice?

This section should have been relatively easy and if not, well at least you know now. The next page delves deeper into areas that either of you have refrained from discussing or it just never came up during a drunken night in.

Going deeper

In this section, questions will relate to things you have maybe never considered to discuss or crossed your mind.

<u>Surprise Gifts</u>
<u>The rules</u>

Everyone loves to get surprised but how you value the gifts can play an important role in future surprises. Do women really love flowers? Do men enjoy silver cufflinks? Does anyone actually enjoy photoframes?

Rate the following gifts out of 1-10, 1 being your favourite and 10 least. Compile the results into a list and share your thoughts.

1. Is sexy Lingerie a nice surprise?

2. How about a nice meal out?

3. A handmade present such as a sketch, card or even a balloon with your face drawn on it?

4. What about receiving some money?

5. A new puppy or pet?

6. A playlist of music only for you?

7. Buying each other gifts together?

8. Coupons for holistic therapy such as Yoga lesson, acupuncture or massage?

9. A surprise getaway?

10. A raunchy boudoir photo session?

Past online dating and social media

The following questions relate to things experienced online or things done online. When asked the question your partner has 90 seconds to think of a reply. If the question doesn't relate to them, then try make an assumption or guess.

1. Received a random private message on fb from a sexy stranger? What did it say?

2. Swiped right on a tinder profile that shows a mutual friend?

3. Found you got added on snapchat by a stranger? What did they want?

4. Have you ever stalked a Facebook account before going on a date?

5. Felt attracted to someone through a forum even though you don't know what they look like?

6. Exchanged nudes? What were they?

7. Found someone who's already in a relationship on a dating app, what did you do?

8. Send flirtatious emails? To whom?

9. Skyped someone you talked with on a dating site? Did you show a little skin?

10. Got excited that a hottie started following you on Instagram? Did you send them a message?

11. Used Facebook to state you are in a relationship?

12. Took the perfect profile picture?

13. Used emojis on your dating profile?

14. Shared nostalgic photos to a stranger?

15. Taken a gym selfie?

16. Met someone through craigslist and not to buy

something?

17. Noticed someone you've seen online in person?

Did you say hi?

18. Kept an ex-partner on your friends list so you can make them jealous?

19. Wrote a FB status about an ex-partner? What did you write?

20. Delete your social media accounts because of someone? Who was it?

With Thought

The rules

This quiz is about things in your relationship that really highlight the intimacy between you both. Decide on how many times each one occurs and whether there needs more involvement or if your relationship is adequate enough.

1. How often do you hug each other?

2. Do you receive encouraging notes such as leave out the garbage?

3. Do you spend one on one time on a daily basis?

4. How often do you get or receive a gift?

5. How about practical help with a challenging task?

6. Do you often hold hands or hug in public?

7. Have a long, deep discussion about a particular

    topic?

8. Tell each other words of affirmation or

   inspirational quotes?

9. Complement each other or give good advice?

10. Just sit around and relax quietly together?

Life goals

After you and your partner have answered each question, place the questions from 1-20 in order of importance, 1 being most important and 20 least. Plot twist; this compiled list is what you think your partner would have chosen. Exchange notes afterwards to see if you have similar viewpoints.

1. How important is planning for retirement?

2. Would you consider moving cities or countries?

3. Have you ever wanted to start a business? What kind of business if so?

4. Go travelling for a few months? Where would you go?

5. Learn to play an instrument and/or start a band?

6. Ever consider volunteering with an organization?

7. Skydiving, bungee jumping or any other extreme sport?

8. Enter a competition that involves one of your hobbies?

9. Would you ever consider changing careers in the future?

10. Do you plan on having kids? How many?

11. Learn to speak another language?

12. Go on an unplanned road trip?

13. Go vegetarian for a month?

14. Lose weight or build some muscle?

15. Run a marathon or do a color run?

16. Write a book, make some art or any other creative

    activity?

17. Learn a new skill for secondary income; think massage therapy, yoga instructor, dance instructor.

18. Meet a famous person, who would it be?

19. Go on a reality TV show? Which show?

20. Star in a movie? What movie would you want to

    appear in?

<u>Sexy minds</u>

<u>The rules</u>

Learning about the way your partner thinks can shed a light into discovering common interests though it could also show they might have a naughty mind too. Ask each question to your partner where they have to finish the sentence. Both of you count to three and then tell each other your answer.

Some crazy questions have been thrown in for entertainment.

1. When a lover recites poetry, it feels

   _____.

2. Having an in-depth and revealing conversation

   is_____.

3. Talking about past sexual encounters is

   _____ to me.

4. An intellectual debate in a relationship teaches me

   that _____.

5. Making you blush is _____ because

_____.

6. If you are shy about sex, I will _____.

7. If I taught you how to make love differently, I

think that you would _____.

8. If I was to think of the sexiest thing we've done, its

_____.

9. If somebody else flirted with me in a club, I think

you would_____.

10. My favourite night with you was when we

_____.

11. I think you would love it if I _____ during

sex.

12. One way I always think about you is by

_____.

13. I like to sometimes imagine you _____

when I arrive from work.

14. I sometimes dream that we _____ inside

IKEA.

15. I discovered a love for gardening after watching

you _____.

16. I want you to order a pizza for me, the toppings I

want are _____.

17. If I was assigned to a Hogwarts house in harry

potter, it would be _____.

18. If I had a band or song I secretly listen to, it is

_____.

19. Sometimes when you not home I watch

_____ on TV.

20. I had to borrow your _____ to scare away wild chickens from the yard.

Anniversary

The rules

If you have already celebrated your anniversary then congratulations, if not then don't worry, it's coming. Since an anniversary is an important time for any relationship, deciding how to captivate the moment is where couples struggle. In this quiz, you and your partner must plan how you will spend the joyous occasion after answering the questions. For example:

Morning: question 1, 2, 4
Afternoon: question 3, 5, 6
Evening: 8, 7, and 9
Night: 10

1. Could you spending some time with no

    technology?

2. Go on a drive through a beautiful countryside?

3. Would you write down a romantic story about how

    you met?

4. Book a hotel for a bit of much needed privacy?

5. Get a tattoo that represents your partner?

6. Go to the first place you both met?

7. Hiring a photographer to take a few photos?

8. Get a couple's massage or take a cooking class together?

9. Allowing your partner to try a new position such as up the butt?

10. Being whisked away on a surprise trip?

The future

Ah if only we could see into the future. Ask the questions to each other and after each answer, separately rate the question from 1- 10, 1 being least important and 10 the most.

1. Can you avoid flirting with a stranger if your

   partner isn't there?

2. Where would be the perfect location to get

   married?

3. What would you consider naming your first son

   daughter?

4. If you could retire in any country, would it be?

5. What's the next biggest plan for your relationship?

6. If there was somewhere special to you that you

   would love your partner to see, where would it be?

7. Would you prefer going on a cruise or travelling

   for a few months with your partner?

8. Does your partner know all of your friends?

9. If you could only bring two people to your wedding, who would it be?

10. Are you going to raise kids under your religion?

11. Is it important for kids to understand religion or better to make a chose when they are adults?

12. Would you leave your partner if they ever had an

    affair?

13. Name 3 rules to give your children?

14. What would you teach your kids about life?

15. How would you propose to your partner if you

    haven't already?

16. If you could go on honeymoon to somewhere no-one else has been, where?

17. Do kids learn more from their parents or from

    school?

18. If a friend or family member couldn't have kids, would you (or if it's your partner) consider being a surrogate?

19. Would you change your political view for your

    partner?

20. Where do you both see each other in 5 years?

Situational, strange and shocking

Places you like to go

The rules

Making out is great but what can make it even more fun? The location. For this quiz, both you and your partner should answer the questions and when finished decide on which 3 locations are the best to spend time together and why.

1. Getting tipsy together at a bar?

2. Making out or having sex in the ocean?

3. During a firework display?

4. During a desert sunrise/sunset?

5. Kissing outside in the middle of a rain storm?

6. Kissing under the stars?

7. Making out in a private pool?

8. Having sex in someone else's house or bed?

9. Sucking face at a gala or costume party?

10. In the middle of a lake?

Work related

The rules

Multiple answer round; Both of you choose one answer for each question and find out who's more risky in the relationship. Don't forget to explain your answer!

1. Would you ever flirt during an interview?

    a) If I get the job, yes.
    b) Absolutely not, especially if the boss looks like a sundried prune.
    c) Maybe, money talks.
    d) Other, your answer.

2. Have you ever considered calling in sick to spend time with you partner?

    a) Yes, what's one day off going to affect my job.
    b) No but it's a good idea.
    c) Maybe, depends if my partner makes it work my while.
    d) Other, your answer.

3. Would you ever bring your partner to work afterhours to make passionate love?

    a) Absolutely, I even have a chair that rotates 360.
    b) No, it's too mundane and boring there.

    c) Maybe, if our house was being renovated or some other reason.
    d) Other, your answer.

4. Have you ever stolen something from work?

a) Yes, it was a _____.
b) No way, I work with _____.
c) Maybe, it depends on _____.
d) Other, your answer.

5. Ever watched porn during work hours?
    a) Yes, it was a celebrity sex tape.
    b) No, who does that?
    c) Maybe, I clicked by accident.
    d) Other, your answer.

6. If you hate your job, what would be a cool way to get fired?

a) Telling the boss what I actually think of them
b) Photocopying your ass and then distributing around the office
c) Convincing everyone else to join you and storm out like an army
d) Other, your answer.

7. What would you do if someone at work was making your life hell?

a) Sit them down and resolve the problem professionally.
b) Warn them that you have incriminating evidence against them.
c) Tell a senior manager about the problem
d) Other, your answer.

8. How would you pass time at a boring work-related event?

   a) Get drunk and dance.
   b) Sit with peers and listen to gossip.
   c) Greet older more high-ranking co-workers in the hope of a promotion.
   d) Other, your answer.

9. If you could change career, how long do you think it would take to transistion?

a) 2 weeks
b) 2months
c) 2 years
d) Other, your answer.

10. How far do you think your partner would go to help you get your dream job?

   a) Work 2 jobs so you can focus better.
   b) Help you write your resume, emails and other communications.
   c) Sacrifice their hobbies to support you.
   d) Other, your answer.

Sex in public

The rules

Look through the questions with your partner, both of you can only answer with "tried it", "Consider it" and "no way hose."

1. Having oral sex in the movie theatre.

2. Allowing someone to watch you both have sex.

3. Oral sex while driving.

4. Having sex in a park (maybe it's a cold night).

5. Making out in a dressing room in a store.

6. Feeling each other up on the dance floor.

7. Not wearing underwear in public.

8. Broadcasting sex on a webcam.

9. Getting dirty while you are babysitting for

   someone.

10. Getting to 2nd, 3rd, 4th base in a swimming pool even if there is people around.

Breaking the rules

The rules

Work as a team and look through the questions. You have decide who is more likely to have either done this before, consider doing it or both.

1. Have you ever brushed up against a stranger sexually?

2. Made out in an elevator?

3. Arousing partner in a public place? Maybe a church?

4. Sex in an office? Using a spinning chair? Against the employee of the month wall?

5. Had sex in a club or bar toilet?

6. Sex on an airplane? Would you want to?

7. Licking chocolate or whipped cream off a partner's body?

8. Wearing a partner's underwear

9. Having sex in someone else's bed?

10. Throwing a used condom out the window in the heat of

the passion?

Slightly Awkward questions

The rules

Read the list of questions together and then both of you make a list about whether you think your partner had done it before or not. Don't show each other until you have finished the list.

1. Skinny dipping at night?

2. Visited a nude beach?

3. Swingers club?

4. Going to a spa and have sex?

5. Buying a sex toy?

6. Staying at a love hotel?

7. Watch someone have sex from outside your window or just be a general pervert?

8. Masturbate in the dark?

9. Watched a stripper/ had a lap dance?

10. Using a fake name when you've met someone?
    What was the name?

More Serious questions

The rules

Each person must answer each question honestly, there are 30 questions in total. Answers should be noted down and then compared at the end.

1. What is the ideal number of calls a couple should exchange in a day?

2. How far are you willing to compromise your happiness for the success of the relationship?

3. What's your idea of a romantic vacation?

4. What do you think is the single most important thing for a relationship to be successful?

5. What do you think defines cheating?

6. If I cheated on you, would you ever forgive me?

7. Would you tell me you were sorry to me even if it's not your fault?

8. Are you friends with any of your exes?

9. How in your relation would you plan your finances?

10. Is Valentine's Day too cheesy?

11. How would you tell your partner you need a break?

12. What was your first impression about me?

13. Are you able to avoid flirting if someone attractive flirts with you when I'm not around?

14. Are romantic gifts memorable or carry any value?

15. If someone close to your partner died, how would you comfort them?

16. What is the most special memory that you hold with your partner?

17. If I told you to jump off a tall cliff and then tell you that you'll land safely as there's a net you can't see, would you blindly trust me and jump?

18. Do you have to know all of my friends?

19. Do you think that past relationship secrets should always be kept hidden?

20. Do you think confessions make a relationship stronger?

21. Is it ok for a partner to use the toilet while the door is open?

22. If we went to a store to buy a rug and both of us liked different rugs, would you still go with the one I picked?

23. Is sex about constantly pushing the boundaries or playing by the rules?

24. How often would you want to go out on a date with your partner in a month?

25. What do you find sexiest about a person of the opposite sex?

26. What's your wildest sexual fantasy that you'd want to try with your partner?

27. Would you feel insecure if your partner spent a lot of time at work?

28. How many sexual partners have you had in the past?

29. If you were convinced that I was making a bad decision, what would you do about it?

30. When was the last time you disliked me?

Hobbies, interests and scary stuff

Beneficial hobbies

The rules

Hobbies are an important part of life, they can keep you sane from a stressful job or keep us entertained. In this quiz, ask each other which of the following questions that appeal to them. At the end of the quiz, decide which three hobbies you will do when you both have free time.

1. Would you draw your partner naked during a

   figurative drawing class?

2. Is going to Zumba with your significant other fun

   or too much?

3. Do you like the idea of being cradled with your

   lover while making pottery?

4. Practice sparring each other in a kung-fu lesson or

   other form of self-defence?

5. Discussing ideas for a story in a creative writing class or just listening to each other's scribbles?

6. What language would you practice with your partner?

7. Who in your relationship would be most eager to learn playing an instrument? Could your partner teach you?

8. Has the idea of growing your own produce in your garden ever come to mind? Would your partner be interested too?

9. Do you think you or your partner has what it takes to perform stand-up comedy on stage?

10. Would you attend a slam poetry night or encourage your partner to?

11. Who would benefit from mediation more in your relationship?

12. What cuisine would you both want to learn the most?

13. Would you both attend a salsa class and then dance in public?

14. Who would most likely catch more Pokémon during a game of Pokémon go?

15. Would you both think about indoor Rock climbing if given the opportunity?

Travel bucket list

Everyone wants to travel but due to obligations, fears or laziness, they never bother.
For this quiz, you and your partner should look through the questions and answer them together.

1. Would you rather learn to cook Thai food or walk through the Great Wall of China?

2. Where would be the first country you would want

   to visit?

3. Name a country in Europe that you wouldn't want to visit and why

4. Which of the following is your partner mostly likely interested in-

   a) Taking photos on a safari
   b) Skiing at a resort
   c) Lying on a beach
   d) Partying on a rooftop bar
   e) Trek through a jungle

5. Which is more important, big ben or statue of

   liberty?

6. What's the best way to spend time on an

   international flight?

7. What language do you think is the hardest to

   speak?

8. What language have you always wanted to learn?

9. What's one country you would never want to visit?

10. Would you ever ride an elephant?

11. Would you and your partner prefer to stay at a party hostel, hotel or a homestay?

12. Would your partner wish to visit every continent in their lifetime?

13. What are 3 things you would always vary with you while travelling?

14. How long would you and your partner travel for?

15. What might be the biggest concern while

travelling?

Seasonal holidays and events

The rules

How does your relationship different during the seasonal holidays or any major events in general? Have a look at the questions and compare answers at the end.

1. Would you pretend to be ill so you and your partner can miss thanksgiving?

2. So you dress sexy, scary or silly on Halloween?

3. Do you prefer xmas dinner at your parents or your partners parents?

4. Have you ever drank green beer on St Patrick's Day?

5. Would you kiss a stranger on New Year's Eve if you were single?

6. Have you ever went on a tinder date on Valentine's Day?

7. What's the most annoying thing about Valentine's

   Day?

8. Would you ever contemplate surprising your partner
   with a trip to the circus?

9. What's the sexiest present you ever got on Christmas?

10. Do you enjoy watching fireworks with your partner on
    Independence Day or any other event?

<u>Scary things</u>

<u>The rules</u>

Knowing each other's fears in a relationship allows for a deeper connection. For this quiz, read the questions to each other. Decide on who wants to answer the question first for each question.

1. Does your partner have an irrational phobia?

2. What would your partners legacy be when they died?

3. Has your partner ever written a will?

4. Could your partner cope with being famous and would it change them?

5. What's the scariest thing your partner has ever told you?

6. Has your partner ever seen a ghost?

7. What does your partner think happens after death?

8. True/false? Your partner finds it hard to talk about

   deceased ones.

9. Which of the following does your partner think **could**

   exist?

a) Witches
b) Ghosts
c) Zombies
d) Vampires

10. Is your partner afraid of death?

11. When was the last time you talked to your partner
    about something that scared you?

12. What is the scariest movie you watched together?

13. When was the first time you were scared?

14. What do you normally do when you are scared with

    your partner?

15. What's the scariest thing about being a teenager?

16. What's your biggest worry about your job?

17. How would you scare your partner as a joke?

18. Did you ever watch something accidently online that traumatised you?

19. Have you ever been threatened or didn't feel safe?

20. If you called your partner and told them you were being followed in the middle of the night, what might they say?

Pet peeves and habits

The rules

Answer each question separately and then count up which you think apply to you and which to your partner.

1. Has your partner ever woke you up from snoring?

2. Have you had to sleep in another room because of your partners snoring?

3. Have you ever had a serious talk about arriving late?

4. Have you ever been loudly woken up by your partner doing house work?

5. Does your partner steal the blanket during the night?

6. What was the last movie you watched in which your partner talked throughout?

7. What do you do when your partner falls sleep on the

   sofa?

8. Do you always get distracted by electronic devices or is it your partner?

9. Has your partner ever borrowed your razor or anything else without telling you?

10. Have you ever disguised an empty carton in the fridge instead of throwing it away?

11. Do you get annoyed if your partner squeezes the middle of the toothbrush tube?

12. Have you ever been told to stop chewing so loudly?

13. What steps have you taken to prevent or lesson a common habit?

14. Do you ever smoke then try and kiss your partner?

15. How many empty glasses are next to your bed at night?

16. What would you do if your partner was rude to a waiter?

17. What does your partner do to make amends when they have pissed you off?

18. Does your partner take out the garbage or you?

19. Does your partner lose keys or do you?

20. What's the most annoying thing your partner does

before bed?

Sexy time

Keeping it sexy

The rules

Keeping the passion in your relationship is important, have a read of the questions, answer them and decide which you might consider to try.

1. Dressing up for each other?

2. Watching a sexy movie in your bedroom together?

3. Going on a second honeymoon?

4. Giving each other provocative looks to get in the

   mood?

5. Getting a babysitter and going to a hotel for the

   evening?

6. Going on a couples retreat?

7. Having a secret locked drawer or closet for sex toys or play things?

8. Taking a morning shower together?

9. Taking a sex class to learn a new technique?

10. Being flirty in front of others?

Foreplay

The rules

How do you get your partner in the mood? Ice-cubes on the nipples? A dramatic reading of fifty shades of grey?

Look through the questions and decide which your partner might consider to try and ones that they wouldn't.

1. Teasing a partner so that they are begging you to have sex with them?

2. Tearing off or having your clothes ripped off?

3. Shaving each other?

4. Having your genitals touched over your clothes?

5. Playing with nipples?

6. Wrestling naked?

7. Being tickled or tickling your partner?

8. Setting the mood with candles?

9. Getting tied up?

10. Using ice cubes?

Sexy talk

The rules

Read the following questions and start to tell the answer with your partner with "I wish you would…" or "I wish you wouldn't…"

1. Saying how much you want each other?

2. Swearing during sex?

3. Saying "I love it when you do that to me"?

4. Whispering in each other's ear?

5. Explaining into the details of a fantasy you're playing out in your head?

6. Telling your partner what they plan to do to them?

7. Being surprised by something your partner says?

8. Hearing oohs & ahhs during love-making?

9. Using funny or pet names for each other?

10. When your partner lets you know they are about to

cum?

Roleplay

The rules

Answer the questions below and choose 3 that you would consider with your partner and then compare.

1. Creating a Top 10 list of celebrities/athletes you'd want to have sex with?

2. Being a porn star for the night?

3. Sharing your sexual fantasies with each other?

4. Going to a themed or costume party?

5. Police or military role play?

6. Pretending you are either a virgin or seducing a virgin?

7. Doctor or nurse/patient role play?

8. Being a slave for a night?

9. Pretending you are having an illicit affair with your

   lover?

10. Pretending you are having sex with a celebrity?

The wild card
Drinking games

Everyone loves drinking games but are there ones that you have never played? Look through the questions and make a promise to your partner that you will play one at some point.

1. Ever played jenga drunk?

2. Spin the bottle with a few friends?

3. Ring of fire with a large group?

4. Is playing never have I ever for kids?

5. Would you play strip poker with strangers?

6. Who is better at beer pong?

7. Ever played most likely?

8. Can you handle the Roxanne drinking game?

9. Twister but drunk?

10. Do you get competitive during flip cup?

Celebrity status, movies and TV

The rules

We live in world where celebrities are everywhere. Look at the questions and answer them while doing a celebrity impression.

1. Have you ever slept with someone who looks like a celebrity?

2. Who would you French kiss if they were A-list famous?

3. Have you ever convinced someone you were famous?

4. Which rock band would you love to party with?

5. Who do you follow the most online?

6. What was the last album you bought?

7. Have you ever considered auditioning for a movie?

8. If you could star in one movie, what would it be?

9. Which friend's character do you resent the most?

10. Do you still watch cartoons? Which ones?

11. Do you think star wars is overrated?

12. What's the best Disney movie?

13. Who would play you in a movie?

14. What's the worst movie you have ever seen?

15. Is your partner able to do a Chewbacca

impression?

16. Which movie series should stop making sequels?

17. Have you ever read an autobiography? Who?

18. Who's the best writer in your opinion?

19. If you were to direct a movie, what kind of movie

would it be?

20. Name a famous funny actor that you don't find
    funny.

21. When was the last time you walked out of a movie
    theatre?

22. What was the last movie you recommended to
    your partner?

23. Do you read reviews before seeing a movie or just
    go see it?

24. Which celebrity do you predict will die soon?

25. Have you ever met someone famous?

26. Do you know anyone famous?

27. If there should be a remake for a movie, which

movie should it be?

28. Which band would be the soundtrack to your life?

29. When was the last time you went to a concert?

    Who was it?

30. If you could bring a famous person back to life, who would it be?

Taboos

The rules

Look through the questions separately and decide on whether it's something you've done, consider doing or would never do.

1. Getting your nipple pierced?

2. Getting a neck tattoo?

3. Getting a tattoo on your bum?

4. Shaving your head for charity?

5. Having your front bum waxed in front of a family member?

6. Doing a prank call to a neighbour?

7. Making a YouTube video that explains multiple orgasms than uploading onto your social media?

8. Stealing food from an all-you-can-eat buffet?

9. Giving a policeman a fake name?

10. Buying alcohol for minors?

11. Throwing a soap on the rope out the window of a car?

12. Taking a dump on the street if you really needed to?

13. Pretending to be pregnant or ill to not pay for something?

14. Sneaking into a cinema without paying?

15. Stealing someone s deodorant in the gym?

16. You find a mannequin on the street, would you take it home?

17. Picking up the neighbour's dog poop and throwing it on their door?

18. Going hunting and making a kill?

19. Buying your partner a douche?

20. Pretending to be asleep on a beach so you don't have to talk to someone?

Who does it better?

The rules

This quiz is to determine who is better at something in your relationship. Ask each question and decide who is better.

1. Making breakfast in bed?

2. Giving advice on work-related issues?

3. A foot massage before bed?

4. Cleaning the bathroom?

5. Making delicious cocktails?

6. Taking the best photos?

7. Playing a board game?

8. Making snacks for a movie night?

9. Deciding on what to bring to a picnic?

10. Giving hugs on the sofa?

11. Thinking of a witty remark?

12. Who's bubblier during a social gathering?

13. Who can handle their booze?

14. Recommending a good place to hang out?

15. Helping out others?

16. Driving a car?

17. Parking the car?

18. Getting everything from the shopping list?

19. Encouraging you with your hobbies?

20. Allowing each other some space to see friends?

Made in the USA
Coppell, TX
08 December 2019